WORKING FOR SOCIAL JUSTICE

APPRECIATING DIVERSITY

Rita Santos

Enslow Publishing
101 W. 23rd Street
Suite 240
New York, NY 10011
USA
enslow.com

Published in 2020 by Enslow Publishing, LLC.
101 W. 23rd Street, Suite 240, New York, NY 10011

Library of Congress Cataloging-in-Publication Data

Names: Santos, Rita, author.
Title: Appreciating diversity / Rita Santos.
Description: New York : Enslow Publishing, 2020. | Series: Working for social justice | Includes bibliographical references and index. | Audience: Grades 3-6.
Identifiers: LCCN 2018047377| ISBN 9781978507852 (library bound) | ISBN 9781978507951 (pbk.) | ISBN 9781978507968 (6 pack)
Subjects: LCSH: Toleration—Juvenile literature. | Cultural pluralism—Juvenile literature. | Multiculturalism—Juvenile literature.
Classification: LCC HM1271 .S3685 2020 | DDC 305.8—dc23
LC record available at https://lccn.loc.gov/2018047377

Printed in the United States of America

To Our Readers: We have done our best to make sure all website addresses in this book were active and appropriate when we went to press. However, the author and the publisher have no control over and assume no liability for the material available on those websites or on any websites they may link to. Any comments or suggestions can be sent by email to customerservice@enslow.com.

Photo Credits: Cover, p. 1 William Perugini/Shutterstock.com; pp. 5, 21 Monkey Business Images/Shutterstock.com; p. 6 Zurijeta/Shutterstock.com; p. 9 espies/Shutterstock.com; p. 10 Hasnuddin/Shutterstock.com; pp. 11, 14 Rawpixel.com/Shutterstock.com; p. 16 Pierre Jean Durieu/Shutterstock.com; p. 17 fasphotographic/Shutterstock.com; p. 19 Africa Studio/Shutterstock.com; p. 22 Andy Dean Photography/Shutterstock.com; p. 24 Creatista/Shutterstock.com; p. 25 Iakov Filimonov/Shutterstock.com; p. 27 Gabriel Olsen/FilmMagic/Getty Images; p. 28 © iStockphoto.com/monkeybusinessimages; cover graphics Stankovic/Shutterstock.com.

CONTENTS

INTRODUCTION

There are close to eight billion people living on Earth. Of that eight billion, no two people are exactly alike. Even identical twins, people who have the exact same genes and look alike, have different likes and dislikes. These differences are called **diversity**. But diversity is about more than just what you look like. Our **cultures** are diverse as well.

Culture is all around us, from the clothes we wear to the food we eat. Even the way we greet each other is cultural. In the United States, you may say hello by giving someone a hug or a handshake. In China and Japan, you would bow when you meet someone. In Portugal, Spain, and France, you'd say hello with a kiss on the cheek. These greetings may all be slightly different but they still impart the same message: that someone is happy to see you. These different greetings are a form of cultural diversity. Your culture is a part of you.

On your very first day of school, you were probably nervous about all the new people you would meet. What if no one liked the same things as you? Or worse: what if they were mean? However, as the school year went on, those fears probably went away as you got to know your classmates. You may not

The world is filled with people of all different races, ethnicities, religious backgrounds, and beliefs.

A person's culture can shape all kinds of things in their life, including what they eat!

like every kid in your class, but once you got to know them they stopped being scary.

In the same way that you were once scared to meet your classmates, some people are scared of people from other cultures. Their traditions, customs, and languages may seem very different. But the more we learn about other cultures the less different they seem. In the same way that your classmates became less scary once you knew them, when you appreciate diversity, the world becomes less scary, too.

one

DIFFERENT FAMILIES, DIFFERENT RULES

Every family has its own set of rules and routines that they follow. You may belong to a family that takes their shoes off when they come inside or that eats pancakes for dinner. Different families have different rules.

The things that make us different from some people make us similar to other people. If you've lived in one place your whole life you probably have a lot in common with your classmates. You speak the same language as most of the people in your town. Your families shop in the same stores. You attend the same school.

Our backgrounds and family traditions can play an important role in who we are. Not all families are the same, but we can often find things we have in common.

Life for a child growing up in another country probably seems very different from your life. But some things are the same. In most countries, you would still have to go to school. Your parent or guardian would still tell you when to go to bed or to do chores.

Every community has its own rules. While some cultures may have customs that are very different from yours, their core values are probably very similar to your own. Communities all over the world value family, education, and safety, just like yours does!

DIVERSE IDENTITIES

Your **identity** is made up of all the different things that make you who you are. Your race, ethnicity, and sex are all identities

Religious practice is just one part of a person's identity.

Discrimination

Some people face **discrimination** for one or more aspects of their identity. When people are discriminated against it means they are being treated unfairly because of who they are. An act of discrimination can be as small as saying something mean about a person's race or gender. Discrimination is always wrong. When a government creates laws that discriminate against people, like when LGBTQ people were not allowed to marry people of the same sex, it's called **oppression**.

Discrimination means mistreating someone based on a part of their identity, like race or sexual orientation.

you're born with. The amount of money your family makes and whether your family believes in a religion or not are also a part of your identity. All of these things combine to make us unique individuals. These identities affect us in different ways. This is known as **intersectionality** because it deals with the many ways communities can intersect and combine.

Everyone experiences the world in different ways. A black woman and an Asian woman may share similar experiences as women but they have different racial experiences. In the same way, a black man and a black woman have similar racial experiences but different gender experiences. There are many ways to be but there is no one "right" way to be.

You are a product of a diverse world. Humans aren't the only different ones. Diversity is a part of nature. There are over 300 breeds of dogs. We can grow over 150 different species of roses. If you wanted to learn every language spoken on Earth today you'd learn more than 6,500 different ways to say "hello." All of these differences make the world a more interesting place.

two

Everyone Deserves Respect

When a friend comes to visit, you probably want to show them your favorite toys and games. If your friend were to tell you they thought your favorite toy was dumb, you'd probably feel bad. Your friend is being very disrespectful to you. When we **respect** others it means we value their feelings. Respect means we treat the things that are important to others with respect even if those things don't have the same importance to us.

It's fun to learn more about different cultures. People love to share things that are important to them with others. As we learn more about people who are different from us we must be careful to treat their cultural and religious traditions with respect.

Even though we're not all the same, we can still have fun together and respect each other.

Practice Respect When Sharing Culture

Among many Native American tribes from the plains, war bonnets are considered to have great cultural and spiritual significance. Members of the tribe must earn the right to wear them, often through acts of bravery in war. People of all cultures appreciate the beauty of these bonnets. Occasionally people who are not members of any plains tribes will wear war bonnets as part of a costume or festive wear. This is disrespectful to the tribes, which consider them sacred. These pieces of clothing are not meant to be used just for a "dress up" game or party. This kind of mistake is called **cultural appropriation.**

There's nothing wrong with borrowing from other cultures if it's done with respect. If you want to wear something from another culture, learn about its cultural importance first. Many traditions and customs are meant to be shared by anyone, but some are meant only to be viewed with respect.

MAKING MISTAKES

It's easy to become defensive when someone tells us we hurt their feelings. Mistakes are hard to admit, especially when they are mistakes that hurt other people. We think good people don't hurt other people's feelings so we may think that admitting we hurt someone makes us a bad person. But that's not how it works.

When someone says you hurt their feelings they're criticizing *what you said,* not who you are. Accidentally hurting someone's feelings doesn't make you a bad person. In these situations, good people

The Human Condition

No matter who you are or where you come from, you have some things in common with every other human on Earth. These traits go deeper than our culture. You have a birthday. You are constantly growing and getting older. You have hopes and dreams for the future. You need to love and be loved by other people. These are part of something called the human condition. It refers to all the parts of life that are universally true. The human condition is a reminder that for as different as we may seem on the surface, deep down we are all the same.

In Native American culture, the clothing of a tribe is very important. It should not be used as a costume by non-indigenous people.

It can feel bad to make a mistake, but admitting we're wrong and apologizing is the first step to doing better.

know they have to apologize. To do that you have to understand why what you said was **offensive**. Once you know why what you said was wrong you'll be able to understand why your friend was upset. This allows you to apologize sincerely because you understand and take responsibility for your actions. It also means you can avoid accidentally saying hurtful things in the future. It's hard to admit our mistakes, but it always makes us better people when we do.

three

WHEN WE DISAGREE

Sometimes people argue about what is or is not offensive. When someone disagrees with us it can be hard to keep our temper, especially when the disagreement is about something important to us. But when we have disagreements we should try to remember that arguments are unpleasant for everyone. Being upset is not an excuse to be mean or disrespectful to people. You cannot change someone's mind if you're being mean to them.

SEEING THE OTHER SIDE

Rather than resorting to bullying, try thinking about the situation from the other person's point of view. Try to see the reasoning behind their opinion. Think about all the different parts of their identity and attempt to figure out how their different identities— their intersectionality—may have shaped their point of view. This process of trying to understand how others think and feel is called **empathy**. It is a sign that we care for others.

Many disagreements come from misunderstandings. Having empathy for others can help us avoid unnecessary arguments. But just because we understand how someone feels doesn't mean we have to agree with them. Empathy helps

We won't always agree with another person's opinion, but we should try to understand their position.

everyone to feel heard and respected even when they disagree.

Most people want to avoid saying offensive things. If someone says something offensive to you or your friends, it's ok to let them know why what they said was hurtful. A person who has empathy will try to see things from your point of view. If the person continues to say offensive things, let them know they are being disrespectful and stop talking to them. You do not have to continue speaking to people who are mean to you. If anyone ever threatens to hurt you or someone you know, tell a trusted adult right away.

KEEPING AN OPEN MIND

Sometimes the hardest part of a disagreement is the moment when we realize we were wrong. No one likes that feeling. But being wrong isn't the end of the world. Everyone has been wrong about something at some point in their life. When we disagree with others it can be a chance to learn something new, but first we have to be able to admit when we're wrong.

Trolling

Making new friends online can be fun, but not everyone online is nice. Some people enjoy saying things to make other people feel bad. These people are called trolls. Some trolls think it's funny to upset people. But no one's laughing at their cruel words. Trolls are bullies. They make the internet unpleasant for everyone.

While the Internet can often be a fun place, be cautious of online bullies, known as trolls.

When we keep an open mind, we can have better and more satisfying talks with each other.

So the next time you find yourself in a disagreement, try to keep an open mind. Allow yourself to consider that you might be wrong. Ask the other person to explain their point of view to you. You might learn something you didn't know before. That information could end up changing your mind. Or it might help strengthen a belief you already have. Being open to being wrong means we're willing to challenge what we believe in order to make sure it's correct.

four

UNDERSTANDING EACH OTHER IS FUN

Things like movies, TV shows, books, magazines, and even video games are all a part of the media. The media is in the business of telling stories. Some stories, like the things you may see on the news or in a documentary, are real. Most stories in the media are fiction meant to entertain us, but they are also meant to represent us. Imagine if someone told a story about you but the story wasn't quite true. Maybe it focused on a very small part of your personality or left out something very important to you. You probably wouldn't like this story very much or feel very respected by the person telling it. Our media can have this effect on groups of people.

The images we see on television and in movies can affect how we see ourselves.

When we see people who are like us in the movies we watch and the books we read, it's called representation. Our media tells us stories about our society, but it leaves many people out of those stories. People of color and people who belong to other minority groups are often excluded from having meaningful roles in books and movies.

MORE, NOT FEWER

Imagine you are playing a video game with your friends. You're about to take your turn when your mom tells you it's time to go. You may have had fun watching your friends play but it would have been

It doesn't make us feel good when we're left out, which is how it can feel for young people of color when they don't see themselves represented.

more fun if you'd been able to play as well. When people lack representation in the media, it's similar to not being able to play the game.

Some people worry that making our media more diverse means their own stories will stop being told. But appreciating diversity means telling everyone's stories. Diversity is about having more stories, not fewer.

Political Correctness

Our language is always changing. New words are made and old words fall out of use all the time. In the past, minority groups were sometimes called by names that are now recognized as offensive. When people stop using a word because it's offensive, it's sometimes said they're being too "politically correct." But imagine that your friend had a nickname they hated. You probably wouldn't refer to them by that name because you care about them. It would also be inaccurate. When we continue to use words or phrases that certain groups find offensive, it is a sign we don't care about how they feel. Choosing the politically correct terms simply shows that we respect people enough to use the correct words.

GOOD REPRESENTATION

But having more stories told about people who share your culture or other kind of identity isn't great if those stories aren't accurate. Most movies about the settling of the American West feature Native

The ABC show *Fresh Off the Boat* is an example of good representation, telling the story of an Asian American family.

Seeing, understanding, and celebrating our differences creates a better world for all of us.

Americans. They are usually seen either peacefully coexisting with white settlers or as threatening villains who want to hurt innocent people. In reality, armies sent to protect white settlers violently drove Native Americans from their homes. Ignoring this traumatic history is disrespectful. Native Americans are represented in these movies but not accurately. For representation to matter it has to be truthful.

When the media tells stories that accurately represent how diverse the world is, it helps everyone feel included. The media can be used to show us all the ways we are unique, and it can remind us of all the things we have in common. Celebrating diversity in our media and our lives makes everyone feel welcome in our communities. When we appreciate each other's differences, the world becomes a friendlier place for everyone to live.

Words to Know

cultural appropriation Misusing a part of someone else's culture.

culture The customs, arts, and social norms of a society, sometimes tied to geography or place of birth.

discrimination When people are treated unfairly because of something they cannot control, like their race or sexual orientation.

diversity When things are different from each other.

empathy Understanding how others feel.

identity Who we are as a person; our likes and dislikes as well as the groups we belong to.

intersectionality The ways in which all the parts of our identity connect and affect each other.

offensive Something rude or upsetting.

oppression Unfair treatment of a group of people who share a common identity by a ruling government.

representation Showing a particular experience or story, usually through film, television or books.

respect Treating others with care.